Still In It To Win It

LYNN MICHELE

Lynn Michele

Footprint Publications

ISBN-10: 1722977183
ISBN-13: 978-1722977184

DEDICATION

I am honored and humbled to dedicate this book to all the precious ones who are currently on their own cancer journey. Your strength, fight, determination, courage and spirit are inspiring beyond words. I am wearing your bracelet if I have one, but these are so much more than just colorful bands with words on them. Instead, these are constant reminders to me to pray for you, cheer for you and think of you! Please know that you never fight alone! #weareone #Godsgotyou

This is obviously just a partial list, but as you see these names, please remember to pray for these amazing warriors!

Kim Thiessen	#toughgirlsfightstrong #allin4Kim
Jan Immel	#prayingforamiracle
Joe Pemberton	#joepstrong #freshoutofbubblegum
Glenn Baker	#inittowinit
Diane Blue	#mommablue
Laura Villareal	#laurastrong
Jack Whitaker	#jacksjourney
Jay Staton	#jaysgotthis
Laura Tipton	
Karen Junkert	
Sarah Justi	
Jack Konrad	
Stephanie Whipple	
Darrell Case	

The next part of my dedication is to all of those we have lost because of cancer. This list grows daily and there is no way to include everyone, but again, here is a partial list of precious people who we miss every day. I continue to tell my story in honor of those who cannot. Yet, they leave a legacy that will live on forever. My heart goes out to each of you who have lost loved ones to this dreaded disease, please know you are in my prayers daily. Please see the lyrics to a song I have dedicated to these amazing people at the end of this book.

Jill, Sherri, Noemi, Patty, Amy, Mike, Brad, Jeff, Gene, Ann, Scott, Barb, Diane, Joey, Mandy, Delene, Anna, Vickie, Chuck, Bula, Jeff, Austin.

I conclude my dedication in honor of those who have walked this journey and are still here, living life in HD, grateful for each extra day and continuing to live their dash! You all are in my heart and I am so thankful for each one of you! I don't have to remind you to live life to the fullest because you are already doing that! I will remind you what I remind myself every day… numbers and statistics are just that, God is God and He is NEVER surprised! He's got us!

#forevergrateful #noonefightsalone

CONTENT

Lynn Michele

ACKNOWLEDGMENTS

I would like to thank some very important people who made this book possible for me:

1. My Heavenly Father ... without Him, none of this is possible and with Him, EVERYTHING is possible.

2. My family for listening to chapters, giving me advice, being patient with me as I write and re-write and for believing in me at all times, I could not do anything I do without you!

3. My brother-in-law, David Lee, for your constant encouragement, unbelievable formatting skills, publishing your book because that gave me the motivation to finish this project, for creating Footprints Publications and so much more.

4. My fearless and ferocious editors: Jan Immel and Sharon Neifer. You ladies are AMAZING and I am so grateful for your editing skills and assistance with this book. I could not have done it without you!

5. Jen Depner, what can I say to you? Your graphic design skills on my cover are nothing short of perfection! Thank you so much for sharing your creative mind with me on this project!

6. My sistas, Patti Tucker, Kim Thiessen, and Sharon Neifer. Your belief in me and constant cheering me on is irreplaceable! #sistas4always

7. To every person who is mentioned in this book, thank you for the enormous impact you have had on my life, God bless you!

INTRODUCTION

What happens after the "hoopla" ceases, the teal ribbons disappear, the multitudes of cards and well wishes stop coming, the inspirational hashtags diminish to mere pound signs and the purple t-shirts are pushed to the bottom of the drawer? What then?

I have written this for all of the "survivors" who are still trying to survive or trying to discern the difference between surviving and thriving. How do we do it?

We try to portray ourselves as constantly joyful. After all, we survived, didn't we? Every day is a blessing so why do some days seem so burdensome?

Hopefully, this book takes on a different enough perspective that it will be an encouragement to all of you who have survived a tumultuous storm, have helped someone who did or who may hear the wind and thunder approaching your own back door!

God is STILL not surprised. The same God, who saw you through the darkest night, will continue to be there when the seemingly clear sky days still are a bit clouded over!

One year later, I'm definitely still in it to win it. Are you?

Lynn Michele

1

I'M CANCER-FREE… NOW WHAT?

The days and weeks following September 5th were a whirlwind. Becoming cancer-free was a day that will always be remembered as a true highlight of my life! It is so amazing to me how going through the initial cancer diagnosis and the shock of it all can be so traumatic, yet moving on can be just as challenging.

I'm cancer-free, so now what? All of the cards, letters, texts, doctor's appointments, Facebook up-dates, countdowns and hashtags come to an abrupt halt! Please don't get me wrong, knowing that God had brought me through my cancer journey was one of the most grateful moments of my entire life! However, I found myself missing those weekly trips to the Cancer Center.

Some of you might already be questioning my sanity. How could I possibly miss any of that? Let me clarify: I did not miss the chemo, the after effects, or waiting anxiously for my most recent CA125 tumor marker number to pop up in my box! What I did miss was seeing my nurses, Dr. Mahdi and all of the people who played such a vital role in my treatments and recovery. I missed seeing them and the reassuring feeling I had every time I left there. I felt safe knowing that I was being thoroughly checked out each week and I had started to rely on that more than I thought possible!

The entire time I was sick, my cousin, Jayne, texted me every single morning. I knew that each time I awoke there would be one, two, or perhaps three text messages from her. Her texts were encouraging and mostly referenced how we were going to continue to kick cancer's butt! It was just such a joy to read those messages! As much as I enjoyed those texts, we knew that when cancer had come to an end, the daily routine of those types of texts needed to end with it. There again, not a sad thing at all, but I had learned to rely on those morning messages of hope and love!

During my cancer journey, my Pops so willingly gave up his recliner to me. From day one, I not only sat in it, I ate in it, and slept in it. It became my "space" which was not always convenient since it sits in the middle of their living room! I also kept in my "space" a collection of cards, journals, books, and other items that were my favorite gifts generously given to me throughout the months. I even kept a stack of stuffed animals beside me on the floor which were gifts, mainly from my nephews.

I will never forget coming home from the center on September 5th and going straight to "my corner" of the living room and cleaning house! I took each item and carefully moved it into my bedroom which had not been utilized except to change clothes in for the past several months! I removed the blanket that had been carefully tucked to cover the recliner every day since my surgery! All of the sudden, my space was dramatically changed back into their living room. Again, a happy day, right? How could a space have become such a "security blanket"? I still do not know *how* it happened, but *it did* happen.

I remember going on a road trip with my parents, only a couple of weeks out of chemo. We decided to take the "I'm Well Tour" and visit our relatives in Kentucky and Tennessee! It was an amazing trip with memories I will treasure for the rest of my life! Yet, as we were settling in at my cousin's home in Kentucky, I distinctly remember feeling a bit lost. She has a very spacious home and we always stay with her when we visit there, a tradition I have come to cherish!

Why did I feel lost? Simply because my bedroom there was at one end of the house and my parent's room was at the other. I vividly recall talking to my Mom privately before we retired the first night asking, " Mom, if I need you, can I text you?" She said, "Yes, honey, you can, this is the farthest you have been from me in quite some time!" The sad reality of this story is that I was genuinely nervous about that first night being "alone" at my end of the house!

I suppose a large part of life after cancer is about embracing the "firsts" that happen and there are too many to even list in this chapter or this book! For me, the initial "first" was our road trip and it was a giant step toward recovery for me!

We scheduled our vacation to begin on September 17th, immediately following my baptism. I had grown up in church and was baptized as a young girl at the Baptist church I attended. I had never doubted my salvation or the decision to be baptized when I was ten years old, but I just really felt a compelling tug at my heart to repeat this public profession of my faith in Jesus. I think a large piece of this was just the fact that I was given a second chance at life and an opportunity to make all things new!

One of the memorable things about this decision was confirmed when Lynn (my chemo nurse turned close friend/family) popped her head in the door during one of my treatments and asked me if I was going to get baptized. She had been considering it herself and wondered if we could take this step together. That was my final confirmation that this was the time for me to take this step!

September 17th was a beautiful fall day. The sky was a spectacular shade of blue and the sun felt so nice and warm. Our church has an annual baptism outside at a quarry in our area and the perfect weather just added to this perfect day! Lynn and I wore my purple "#inittowinit" t-shirts. Two Lynn's, two friends joined together because of cancer, taking this "plunge" together – how much more special could it be! Our pastor, who was talking about each of us as we walked out into the water to get dunked, announced that I was cancer-free. He also explained that Lynn and I met at the Cancer Center because she was my nurse. It was truly moving.

I grabbed Lynn's hand and we walked out into the shockingly COLD water. Thank goodness I had her, I could NOT have trudged through that deep water and sand without her! Our families were there to cheer us on and take pictures afterward. It was a moment that I will always cherish!

After the baptism, my parents and I headed out, my first long road trip since cancer! I was thrilled to help in the task of driving, I LOVE to drive! We visited with my cousins, aunts and uncle. It was an amazing time to get to see family members I had not been able to see since I got sick. The only difficult part of going was knowing we had to leave in a just a couple of days so that we could get to Tennessee. The time seemed to fly by!

Going back to visit our family in the Smokies was such a healing experience for me since the last time I had been there I was sick and could barely survive the few days we had there! Just to be clear, I have the most amazing family, both my Dad's side and my Mom's, absolutely priceless people that I am honored to call family. Our visits with them were perfect. I was also able to meet up with friends whom are like family to me as well. All in all, it was a perfect tour.

I was exhausted driving home, but for the first time in a long time, it was a "good tired". Good because I was tired from spending countless hours with people who mean the world to me! Good because I was not depleted of all of my energy because of chemo or cancer, but because of making lifelong memories with those I love! My first "first" exceeded my expectations by a long shot and I was filled with extreme gratitude!

Despite the steps of faith that life after cancer has forced me to take, the rewards definitely out-weigh the risks! Fears of sleeping far away from my caregivers, feeling anxious because I am not seeing my doctor and nurses every week, the frightful thought of cancer returning as the statistics indicate, or the subtle side effects that still remain that are only indicative of cancer and chemotherapy patients. Not one of these fear factors come close to the complete joy and gratitude that I have every second of each extra day that I have been given!

I am cancer-free… now what? Learning to live again, truly living *the dash*. What is the dash you might ask? Keep reading, you will find out!

2

LIVING MY DASH

I read a poem not very long ago about "the dash". I had never really given it much thought until that beautiful rhyme was brought to my attention. It seems at funerals there is so much importance placed on the date of the loved one's birth and the date they passed away. I understand these are extremely significant time markers, but now I fully understand the importance of that little line in between the two, the dash.

Sitting here today I realize how different my dash would have been if I had not been given this second chance, these extra days! So many people who are diagnosed with advanced cancer do not get this opportunity. These folks are not allowed the chance to say what they wanted to say or do what they always dreamed of doing!

The dash - that line in between our birthdate and the day God calls us home. Just an insignificant little line separating our two most important life events, but just how significant is it? That little line and what we do with it means EVERYTHING! Our dash will be what we are remembered by, what our loved ones will cling to, and what will differentiate a purposeful and meaningful life from one that could have been so much more.

March 3rd, 2017 is a date that should be placed on my head stone some day! This is the date that my "old life" ended and a new one began. Honestly, those two lives are difficult to blend, each one is so distinctly different. The life before my diagnosis was so caught up in the tyranny of the urgent, not always what was vitally important. My second life, my "extra days" encountered a complete make-over!

I hope that I can take the liberty to just use this chapter as a time for us to have "coffee and donuts"! My brother-in-law, David, whom I have mentioned on several occasions, always used that saying when he was the principal of my high school. I always knew I was in some sort of trouble when he would pass me in the hallway and say, "Lynn, meet me in my office for coffee and donuts, we need to have a *loooong* talk!" Just to clarify, typically there was not coffee or donuts at these meetings! Either way, I would like to have one of those chats with you for a few moments!

Some things just do not matter, might we begin here? A large stack of laundry for instance. We can stress about that pile of polyester or we can realize that the people who wear those clothes are the people we could not do without and this task will get accomplished in time. What about a dusty house or a cluttered garage or a car that looks like it has been driven through three tsunamis? At the end of the day, are these things urgent? When people think about your "dash", will laundry, house cleaning skills or a dirty car be the focus of their thought? I highly doubt it. How do I know this? I am so happy you asked!

When I was given my diagnosis of Stage 3 C Ovarian Cancer, my life did pass in front of my eyes in a matter of moments. None of the memories or pictures in my mind were of a clean house, a clean car, or an organized laundry room. The moments that popped up immediately were of family, friends, laughs, hugs, Christmas, birthdays, and so much more… the true definition of *important vs urgent.*

Okay, so we have established some things that are NOT urgent in the grand scheme of things. Now, may we move on to a list of things that ARE important? Ready, set, here is a partial list for you to consider:

1. Pictures. Take as many pictures as possible! Before you comment, it does not matter what your hair or makeup looks like, TAKE THE PICTURE! The purpose of the picture is to capture a moment, not minuscule flaws only seen by you and I! (If adding filters makes you feel better, add away!)

2. Take the long way home. If you have time and you have the option, always take the scenic route! Why? It gives you more time with whomever you happen to be with and adds variety to the mundane.

3. Become a sunrise and sunset chaser! Storm chasing is so 2017… I have been known to go five miles out of my way to be able to have the optimal view of sunsets! If you are blessed enough to chase a gorgeous one down, take a pic and share it! By the way, each sunrise and sunset are beautiful things. One means we have been

given a new day and the other means we have had the honor of being here through another day!

4. Go to programs, plays, games, archery tournaments, any event that involves those you love as participants! Being there to attend these important activities is a reason to celebrate, so do just that, don't just attend, CELEBRATE each one!

5. S-L-O-W   D-O-W-N! Take time to savor moments, not haphazardly rush from place to place or plan to plan without enjoying these moments, places and plans. Every mile is a memory only if you take the time necessary to create those memories!

6. Become an observer!   Observe what? EVERYTHING!   Notice the clouds, the blue skies, the gray skies, lightning and distant thunder before a thunderstorm, listen to the rain, step outside and feel the wind on your face, smell the rose you have passed by fifty times in the past week, watch the cardinals in your backyard, stand in the sunshine, turn off the AC and open the windows. Take time to breathe the air, soak up the sunshine, dance in the rain, sing in the shower, and attempt to fully appreciate the everyday and common things ... before long they won't seem "everyday" or "common" anymore!

7. Share God's goodness with everyone you meet! You certainly do not have to endure cancer to have a story to tell. Each day that we are given is a reason to share God's goodness in our lives with those around us!

8. See your loved ones. See, as in, really know them, know them by heart! What is your daughter's favorite thing to do with you? What is your son's number one team? What makes your mom or dad happy? What color is your best friend's eyes? Do you know? Don't just look at those you love, SEE them!

9. Take time for physical and personal contact! The day and age we live in is so smart phone oriented that we have become "dumb" regarding personal contact with those we love! Make a phone call instead of texting. If you only have a couple minutes, utilize them with your voice verses your text! Stop and surprise someone at work, or at home, just to give them a hug and say "Hi"!

10. Try to prioritize based on what is important, not what appears to be urgent. Priority lists have been an enormous difference maker in my new life, I literally make handwritten notes and number the activities by importance. These lists are excellent reminders to me when my days get busy and bogged down with *urgency* instead of *importance!*

July 16, 1967 - ???? The end number does not matter as much as that seemingly insignificant line in the middle does... I am forever grateful that I have learned to emphatically live out my dash!

3

THE OVARIAN SISTERHOOD

I am learning the art of being observant, not just looking. I am learning to see people and things for what they truly are, not what I perceive them to be. I am also beginning to step into the world of coming out of my box, going where it is not always comfortable and attempting to see the big picture!

Through these perception alterations, I am finally beginning to notice the silver linings in each situation. For example, going through cancer has accomplished some important things with my friendships. I have had the rewarding experience of rekindling and reuniting with friends; that has been amazingly healing! At the same time, I have been introduced to some new friendships that would not have happened without my cancer journey.

I mentioned in my first book about my Ovarian Sisters... little did I know what these new friends would ultimately mean to me! Patti and I were the first ones to find each other at chemotherapy and we established early on that we would refer to each other as "sista". (pronounced sis-tuh)

People think we are legitimate sisters everywhere we go! We did have the same diagnosis, (one week a part) the same surgeon, the same surgery, the same incision, the same scar, and the list goes on. Patti was my mom's hair stylist when I was just a young girl and I always remembered her fondly. It is sad that it took Ovarian Cancer to bring us back together, but we are such close friends and I am forever grateful. Patti = Personality Plus

Next in the Sisterhood was Kim, we found each other when her daughter-in-law came across my blog and recommended it to her. Again, I had known Kim thirty some years prior to our diagnoses. She had her children in the daycare center that my mom administrated and we thought the world of her and her kids! Kim was diagnosed with Ovarian Cancer as well, stage 4. Kim and I were able to talk quite often before she went through her surgery. Kim has one of the most pure and kind hearts that I have ever known. She has encouraged me immensely with her fortitude and fight. It was great to reunite with her, but again, I wish it had been another way. Kim = Kind and Caring Heart

The next sista came along during chemotherapy at the Sandusky Cancer Center. I had been in chemo since April 18th and by the June and July mark I was feeling the Taxol and Carbo effects full force... that is when Sharon came into the picture! I remember seeing her come into the treatment center with her sister. Sharon and Karen, they would quiz each other with trivia questions during Sharon's treatments. I was in awe of her concentration and alertness even after Benadryl was administered! I wish that I would have felt better and had the ambition to get to know her better during our treatment times, unfortunately, I did not. What I did observe from my chemo chair was her heart, compassion and contagious smile! Sharon = Protector and thankfully, the story does not end here...

I was blessed to have a book signing after _In It To Win It_ was published. We were able to have it here in town. Renaissance Salon and Gallery, the home of my amazing hairdresser, Joni. She very graciously hosted this momentous day for me! It was a cold December day and I had no idea who would show up or if anyone would!

It was no surprise when Patti and Kim were my first two to arrive, I was both excited and honored to have them there! A few other friends popped in and it was just one of those days I will remember the rest of my life! It was an enormous surprise when my mom looked out the door and said, "Hey, there is the lady from chemo!" I questioned as to which lady she was referring to. Mom said, "Remember the one who always did trivia questions with her sister?" Sure enough, it was Sharon!

I was humbled, honored and overwhelmed to have my family, friends and the amazing cancer-kicking ladies with me that day! Patti, Kim, Sharon and I all come from different walks of life, different backgrounds, yet all brought together through what could have been the most devastating times of our lives! We had such a great bonding time during that couple of hours at the book signing.

All four of us got together for a group picture before they left and that day will forever stand as the beginning of the Ovarian Sisterhood! A few days later during texting we decided that we needed to get together monthly for dinner. We meet up and laugh, talk, plan, laugh, eat and laugh some more! The other thing we have developed is a daily group text message, this typically begins early in the morning authored by the only one of us that actually enjoys early mornings… Sharon! These texts have become something that I could not imagine my life without, so have the friendships.

Through our gatherings, Patti began telling us about a support group that she attends monthly. The organization who sponsors it is the Ovarian Cancer Connection (OCC). All of us have been so impressed with all of the things that OCC does for survivors of any type of Gynecologic Cancer. We had the privilege of meeting with the founder of this organization, Gini. What an amazing lady! As we met with her, we found out that OCC is there for ladies during chemotherapy by providing gas cards to assist with trips to the doctor and chemo. They also assist with insurance co-pays, utility bills, personal items and local resources.

Patti, Kim, Sharon and I decided we wanted to go a step further and actually start a satellite branch here in Fremont! Gini has assisted us each step of the way. We have a long way to go, but we have had the honor of assisting four ladies with recent ovarian diagnoses. This organization is very near and dear to my heart and I wish I would have known about it when I traveled my journey.

Just pondering all that God has accomplished even through this dreaded disease is almost impossible for me to wrap my head around! The fact that a disgusting disease could be the common denominator that brought our Ovarian Sisterhood together never ceases to amaze me! Now we are actually working together to help others who have to hear this life changing news! Please keep in mind that our group is working with OCC to help others, while we are doing so, Kim is still enduring chemotherapy! The strength and determination that I see in my sistas constantly pushes me to be the best that I can be with each extra day that I am blessed with.

We are actually working together to host the first-ever Ovarian Awareness 5K in Fremont. We will have it on Saturday, September 8th and we cannot wait! All of the money raised at this event will go to the Ovarian Cancer Connection. One of the things we love about OCC is that each and every person who is a part of it is a volunteer, no one makes any money from this at all! Thus, every penny raised for it goes directly to assisting ladies who so desperately need it!

God winks in ways that I will never fully understand, but I am finally learning how to be still, observe and appreciate more than I ever have before! (You want to know more about God winks? Stay tuned!) We can find good and irreplaceable gifts even in the darkest of times if we keep our eyes, hearts and minds open for them. Cancer is NOT the end to my story, it is only the beginning. In addition, cancer is NOT my story, but *merely a chapter within my story.* Most importantly, cancer came to destroy, **but it has not**, it has **deployed**! It has deployed faith, friendships, and a new found love of life! These are the effects of cancer that I long to hold on to for the rest of my life.

4

BUSY BATTLING MY MIND

My mind drifts back to my diagnosis days, my finite memory attempting to re-live those first few minutes and hours. How did I really feel? Where did my immediate thoughts go? Emotionally, what was going on inside me? Then my thoughts turn toward the day of surgery... the frets and fears, anxieties and assumptions, cares and concerns! How about chemotherapy? The first day of treatment how did I feel, what was I most worried about?

The mind is an extremely meticulous organ! What it chooses to recollect and what it sifts and sorts away forever has no rhyme nor reason. No matter how hard I try, I cannot completely recall the events I just mentioned. I cannot remember the way I felt riding home from my doctor's office knowing that I had bilateral ovarian cancer that had metastasized. I honestly cannot go back in time and remember how I felt before cancer. However, I do recall feeling invincible at times and took pride in the fact that I was extremely healthy and strong.

As I now look back on it all, I recall times I felt so weak and weary. There were days I was so sick of feeling sick that I just wanted to throw my hands up in the air and yell, "Forget chemo, I am NOT going back!" At the time, I thought that fighting cancer would be the most difficult struggle I would ever face. Well, guess what? It was not!

During one of my last visits with Dr. Mahdi, he mentioned I was eligible for a Clinical Trial through Cleveland Clinic because of my diagnosis, age and other factors. He went on to explain the entire opportunity to me. As a participant I would have to be seen every six weeks for labs and CT scans and take a prescribed "medication" daily. The "medication" would be either a PARP(Poly-ADPP Ribose Polymerase) Inhibitor or a placebo. PARP is a protein found in our cells which helps the damaged cell repair itself. As a cancer treatment, PARP inhibitors stop the PARP from doing its repair work in cancer cells and the cell then dies. Neither Dr. Mahdi or I would be permitted to know if I was receiving the PARP inhibitor or if I was one of the 50% of the participants receiving the placebo.

I prayed and asked others close to me to pray for peace in my decision to participate or not. After much deliberation, I decided to take part in this clinical trial because I felt it could potentially benefit not only myself but others. I signed the consent forms and took them back in to Dr. Mahdi and was directed to contact the supervisor of the trial as soon as possible.

I remember receiving her phone call and speaking with her at great length about the entire process. All of the sudden, at some point in the conversation, my complete peace left me! There were things about the trial that concerned me such as the fact that if I did receive the "real" medication, it could cause similar side effects to those I had endured throughout chemo. I would also be required to have several more CT scans with contrast, even though the side effects from frequent CT scanning INCLUDES the development of cancer and kidney failure. Additionally, I would have to go to Cleveland every six weeks for the duration of the trial - at least two years. To top it all, there was absolutely zero proof that this trial would bring any benefits to my health whatsoever.

At the end of the conversation with the representative of this trial, I found I had a complete change of heart and mind. All of the peace that I had felt prior to the phone call, completely vanished: In 3 – 2 – 1 , yes, it was gone! I said a quick prayer and asked God to please confirm the validity of these unsettled thoughts I was now having about the trial and verify for me that I had signed the consent form prematurely. When I finished that prayer, an overwhelming sense of peace overcame me and I knew what I needed to do!

I picked up my phone and called the clinical trial number. The same lady I had just spoken with answered and she could immediately tell by my voice that I had changed my mind. She began backpedaling, trying to get me to see the "good" aspects of the trial. My decision was no fault of hers, she was definitely doing her job, but I just knew in my heart that it was not right FOR ME. After I turned down her several attempts to change my mind, we ended the call.

I remember instantly feeling an enormous wave of relief … I was not participating in the trial and I felt nothing but calm in my heart. The next step was to explain to my family why I had a complete change of heart. They were accepting as always and understood my concerns with it. Regarding the clinical trial, I do not want to bore you with the details but for those of you who might be facing this decision in your life, or know someone who is, I will briefly explain my reasons.

First, I had endured five CT Scans with Contrast within six months and those caused extreme stress on my kidneys. The trial would have required several repeat scans. Secondly, intravenous chemotherapy had damaged and depleted my veins. We consider ourselves blessed now to locate a vein stable enough to supply enough blood for the lab work, much less finding a vein able to handle the dye required to perform this scan!. Third, I could end up with the placebo which would mean I was putting myself at risk for serious complications, including another cancer or kidney failure, for naught! Fourth, I wanted to feel "well" again. Going to the repeated appointments would have made me still *feel* sick. Lastly, I did not want to risk feeling the same side effects I had just endured through chemo!

Please note these were MY reasons, based on what was best for ME only! I am in no way downgrading the good that clinical trials can do, nor am I advising anyone else regarding making any similar decisions! I just felt compelled to share this because it is real life and part of my struggle in moving forward.

During my cancer diagnosis, surgery, recovery, chemo and more recovery, my mind stayed extraordinarily strong. I give God, my family and friends – my incredible support system - complete credit for that. The texts, visits, cards, prayers, calls, fundraisers, t-shirts, bracelets, and surprise events kept me going strong! The support I had at the Sandusky Cancer Center was and still is second to none. With all that being said, there comes a time when life has to move on, right?

I have alluded to various endings that should have made me happy, but instead, brought on melancholy moods. For instance, my final appointment with Dr. Mahdi post chemo was a very happy occasion! Yet, after we left that day, I felt very empty and insecure. I knew I would not get the weekly lab work, weekly interaction and reassurance from my medical team, weekly weigh in - you get the point! I went from my life revolving around doctor and chemo visits to not returning for three months!

During my final visit with Dr. Mahdi, he also had to review the statsitical facts and figures with me. He is the most positive doctor I have ever met, and I could tell that this was the least favorite aspect of his job. He left it until the very end of our meeting and he went over it as quickly as possible. As I mentioned in my first book, Dr. Mahdi told me that due to my diagnosis I have a 60-70% chance of getting the cancer back within the first two years. He also stated that he believes I will be in the 30-40% who do not get it back! (Have I mentioned how much my Dr. means to me?)

Going through the clinical trial information and process, they also informed me of some further percentages. I think the most difficult one for me to swallow is that only 39% of patients who are diagnosed with Ovarian Stage 3C live five years beyond their diagnosis! Thirty-nine percent!!! If I am choosing a day to go to the pool, I check out the extended forecast and tend to stay away from days where there is only a 39% chance of sunshine. Makes sense, right?

So what's my point here? What am I trying to say? I am saying that the statistics and percentages are not promising. So each morning when I wake up - before I even get out bed - I thank God for another day, an "extra" day. (This is saying a lot because I am NOT a morning person!) I thank Him for the weather even if it's only 39% sunny, the chance I have been given to breathe the air, the opportunity to have another day with those I love. I even have the habit of singing a powerful praise song all the way to work each morning! This gears me up for my day. I get to work and go about my business ... but almost daily, something will remind me of that silly number. Even though I know it will happen, it still sneaks up on me. Will I beat the odds? Will I be here until I am fifty-five years old? Will my parents have to bury a daughter? What about my kids and grandkids?

See where my mind can go in just a few seconds time? Busy battling my mind, I had no idea how intense this battle would be! I have to be honest; cancer is an ugly monster - one that no one should have to face in their lifetime! But I have come to realize my mind can be a bigger menace than the cancer was! My daily struggle is compounded by the remnants of this disease and its treatment, including regaining complete strength to combat it!

I cannot leave you hanging after these dark and dismal paragraphs. How can this battle be won? It is a daily, sometimes hourly process! Each time a negative thought comes my way, or I start feeling that dooming doubt, I turn to God first! I pray and I quote my verse: Philippians 4:13 – I can do ALL things through Christ Who strengthens me! Then I go to Nahum 1:9 – Whatever you devise against the Lord, He will make a COMPLETE end of it. Distress will NOT rise up twice.

I have found music is such a healer. I have my playlists and I utilize the appropriate ones depending on my mood and outlook. Happy, positive and powerful songs can change my heart which in turn reverses my mind! I will not start listing song titles here there are too many. However, if we ever get to have a one-on-one conversation, I will gladly share the songs that have helped me through!

There is nothing like prayer, however. Prayer = Power! Please do not stop praying for someone because they are cancer free! Take time to praise, absolutely, but I urge you to please continue praying! Cancer is a ferociously fierce foe, without a doubt, but the battle that follows is as well! When someone asks me how I am doing now, my answer is often, "Great, but extremely busy!" I am certain that most people do not understand that by saying "busy", I am referring to being *Busy with the Battle of my Mind*!

5

THE BOOK TOUR

I have always been intrigued by book tours, even if I've never read the book or have a clue who the author is! ! I suppose the biggest reason is because they had the discipline and determination to get their story down on paper. Not only did they get it on paper, but they also had the courage to put it out there for the public to read! I have actually stopped in at a couple different book signings just to see what it was all about.

If you would have told me one year ago that I would have the honor to write a book, I would have been overwhelmed with joy! On top of that, if I could have known that book would lead to a mini book tour, I would never have believed it! Yet here we are one year later and I have a chapter in my second book that is entitled "The Book Tour"! God's goodness certainly surpasses my understanding!

After my book signing, the holidays were upon us. Amidst the hustle and bustle of the Christmas season, I thought the signing was the climax of my first book project, but

God had other ideas! I was thrilled when 13-ABC from Toledo, Ohio volunteered to cover the event in a segment on their six o'clock news and they did a tremendous job, as always!

I remember the first message I received asked me to consider coming to speak at the church's Ladies Night Out event. I was in shock and awe... speak about my book to two hundred ladies? Talk about humbling – this opportunity was just beyond my understanding. I automatically recalled the promise that I had made while laying in my hospital bed in Cleveland Clinic. I vowed if God allowed me to live through this cancer journey, I would accept any opportunity He gave me.

That being said, I agreed to this engagement and began the preparations to speak for ten to thirteen minutes. I found that as I planned out what I was going to share, I painstakingly reached into the depths of my heart and mind to find the most pertinent points to relay in regard to my cancer, my book and my recovery. I will be sharing part of my first talk in one of the final chapters of this book, so stay tuned!

That Ladies Night Out was an amazing evening! There were over two hundred ladies there and I have to admit, I was intimidated! Thank goodness I had note cards. They pulled me through when I wanted to stray or had one of my "squirrel" moments! The most touching part of the evening, however, was the opportunity to talk with those who came up to purchase my book or just to share their stories with me.

That night was the revelation of a new truth to me. There are countless people affected by cancer in one way or another and they are just waiting for the opportunity to talk and share their experiences.

After that first opportunity, two more churches opened up to me for similar speaking engagements. One was during a church service to the entire congregation and yet another at a ladies breakfast. The ladies breakfast was a very intimate talk with all ladies (other than the sound guy) and I was asked to speak for thirty – forty-five minutes. The one common denominator with each of these opportunities was the overwhelming number of people who had cancer, had loved ones with it currently or had lost someone because of cancer.

I almost did not include this chapter because I do not want this book to be about me. I want it to be a testament to God's power, healing and grace. But as I thought about those three things, I discovered this chapter had to be implemented because it perfectly exemplifies all that God can do! You see, cancer came into my life as a dreaded, dooming and disgusting disease with the ultimate desire to take my life! However, God had a much different plan! I firmly believe His plan was to use this desert season in my life for my good and His glory!

I must admit, before cancer hit, I was living life the way I wanted to and feeling like I was in control. I mean, I knew that God was ultimately in charge, but I felt like I was in a good place and was ready to tackle the world! Then out of the blue - the deepest, darkest blue - a bomb was dropped! This is the place that I had to come to. I wish it had not taken cancer to bring me to this realization, but God continues to use this to further His plan for my life!

I can remember as a high school senior writing down a list of goals for myself - one of which was to write a book. I have been an avid writer since I was a kid, yet, until my sickness came, that book did not materialize. In a way, this horrific time opened my eyes in ways that nothing else could have.

So, life after cancer means different things to different people. Some people will write a book, others will share their stories in other way. Some will be bitter, some will be better, yet others will question why. I am not sure where I fit into all of that just yet since I have felt each of these emotions throughout my journey and honestly, continue to do so. But I also know that I will continue to use each second, minute, hour and day as a gift, because it is!

"The Book Tour" is just a short insert to remind myself and my readers that God can use ANYTHING for our good and His glory! God's plans are not my plans, and His ways are not my ways! My short lived book tour taught me more lessons than I could have ever learned otherwise. There is a reason and a season for everything … sometimes, we just have to look more closely to find the silver lining in it all.

6

PICTURES

Memories
are special moments
that tell our
Story

Dr. Mahdi

March 21st 2017   June 15th 2018

My surgery support team, March 14th 2017

(Left) David, Leisha and I at pre-op day at Cleveland Clinic, March 10th 2017 (Right) My brother-in-law, mentor, friend, coach and more

(Left) Jayne and I on the day I met Dr. Mahdi, March 3rd 2017

(Right) My life-long friend and nurse, Sara

(Left) My first chemo April 18th 2017 (Right) My sis and I at my
daughter's wedding, May 27th 2017

At the wedding, Leisha and I doing the dance, Where You Lead, I Will Follow!

My sis and I at the Fourth of July celebration at our parent's
My sister, my hero and friend!

Celebrating my 50th! My heart was full!!!

My surprise 50th from my kids! Ali, Luke, Leisha and Tim

My AMAZING family at the 2017 reunion #casestrong

My cousin, Evan, painted his senior parking spot in my honor... too awesome!

(Left) Christmas in July Surprise with Terri, Eunice and my Momma! July 2017 (Right) My nephew Nathan!

Colty thought of me even on vacation! #inittowinit

(Left) My great nephews and I, Brody and Indy, Christmas 2018
(Right) My life long bff, Mary

My daughter and nieces, Crystal and Cassidy (Roles)

(Left) My mentor and God send friend, Heather
(Right) My nurse, cousin and one of my heroes, Jayne

(Above) Chemo when we were close to the end! My momma and my kid, always by my side! Two of my best friends, supporters and rocks! My daughter and my Momma! (Below) My nurse, friend Lynn and I after getting baptized, September 2017

(Left) My day at The Shoe included attending the Big Nut's tailgate! (Right) My son-in-law, Tim! God bless you son! (Below) Chad, Tracy and I... Chad was the originator of "Don't pass the ball" and "Two more bites!"

My incredible family at Easter 2018!

(Left) One of my God winks friends, Jan
(Right) Dr. Haynes

The day we became sistas!
Sharon, Lynn, Patti and Kim

(Left) The sistas working our OCC table at the survivorship breakfast at
the Sandusky Cancer Center
(Right) Sistas at Relay for Life Survivor Lap 2018!

And YES, I'm a Mi-Mi! May 15th 2018, welcome Emery Rose!

7

#SUNSETCHASERS

Most of my life I had an extreme fear of thunderstorms and tornadoes, seriously afraid of them! I was so intrigued by storm chasers though, people who not only enjoyed storms, but found it thrilling and satisfying to seek them out! Some of the pictures and video footage I have seen, captured by these chasers, are nothing short of breath taking!

As I was pondering all of this, I decided that if there could be storm chasers, why couldn't there be sunset and sky chasers? Instead of hunting down the most dangerous and electrifying storms, why not drive miles out of the way just to find the perfect angle of the most picturesque sunset? As I started doing this and posting my pictures, I realized that more and more people began doing the same thing! I have labeled all of us sky obsessed folks, #sunsetchasers.

I try to embrace each change that my journey with cancer has had on my life, good and bad, after all, I cannot change it, right? As I reflect on some of the blessings, one of them is in regards to the fact that I mentioned a couple paragraphs ago… You see, before cancer, I was petrified of storms! Post cancer, I literally LOVE them! I long for thunderstorms to go to sleep to, the sound of the heavy rain, increasing winds and thunder, these sounds are now like a serene sonnet to me!

Why am I not afraid of storms anymore? I have NO idea! ☺ I find myself reflecting on the things that previously I had fears of, things that seem so insignificant now. My list of items I stress about has reduced exponentially. I am too blessed to be stressed, have you heard that saying before? I have heard it so many times and even quoted it, but I am not sure that I fully believed it until the past year and a half. I am also too blessed to be afraid of thunderstorms! The truth that I am in God's hand and nothing or no one can pluck me out, casts out a multitude of frets and fears.

The fact is, as I process day-to-day life now, it is very different for me. I was diagnosed with Ovarian Stage 3C Cancer, try to scare me now! (insert LOL here) Life is not as scary after you realize how quickly you can lose it, if that makes sense?

Before I received my diagnosis, I had the ideal role model for handling difficult situations. My mom is a pillar of strength, literally, she is the strongest person I know! She has gone through two open heart surgeries and at least four strokes. I thought about saying she "survived" these events, but that would not be even close to the truth! She THRIVED through these catastrophic medical events!

Through my journey with cancer, my mom remained a rock, she helped me and continues to, more than I can express. She definitely demonstrated to me how to get over fears and to focus on what really matters in life. Why do I mention her? Simply because my mom's heart, generosity, strength, courage and love are five things that have played a vital role in me being here… without her, I would not be a sunset chaser.

What makes a person a true member of our newly-formed #sunsetchasers "club"? Let's list a few of the qualifications:

1. You must take time to actually look for the sunsets.

2. You must get in the position necessary to capture the sunset in its most vivid glory. (Even if that means driving five miles out of the way to do so!)

3. You must share these pics via Facebook, text, emails, or all of the above! (A true sunset chaser does so with the intent of sharing it!)

4. You must learn to appreciate each sunset as if it is your first and your last! (Because that is TRUE appreciation)

A little fun fact I have learned throughout this sunset chasing experience is that it does not stop at sunsets; no, definitely not! Sunset chasing is about seeing life in **High Definition**. It is about noticing the seemingly little things that really are not so little. It requires opening your eyes, ears; heck, all of your senses!

I walked out of church last night and noticed a lilac bush beside the building. It has obviously been there for years due to the size of it. As my friend, Heather, and I walked beside it I expressed to her that I had probably walked by that same bush one hundred times, but it never looked as beautiful to me as it did last night! She stopped and smelled it, gave me a hug and thanked me for pointing it out to her.

Speaking of Heather… I need to take a moment to talk about her. We have a mentoring program at our church and hesitantly, I decided to sign up for it this year. You make a six-month commitment to be either a mentee or a mentor. Most of my life I would have been on the mentor side, not this time! I know now that my decision to enter this program (even though I knew I really did not "have time") was one of the best decisions I could have made.

Heather is my mentor, but we saw from day one that we were instant friends. Not just typical friends, but the best kind of friends! One thing she says to me on a consistent basis is "You love well!" I think that learning to love well is another aspect of sunset chasing. Loving well, giving and living with my whole heart is just another aspect of living life in high definition. Loving, sharing and caring intentionally are very important aspects to truly LIVING each day… not just surviving each day!

So, what are other ways that we can be sunset chasers without actually chasing each sunset? Find the brightest star in the brilliant night sky, share that star with someone else. Notice and appreciate the wildlife in your own back yard… we have squirrels, rabbits, cardinals, finches, and so many other birds! We have probably always had these animals, but I did not take time to watch them or enjoy their presence until the past eighteen months! The funny thing is, as I anxiously wait to see them in the yard, my parents are not as happy due to the fact that the cute little guys enjoy their garden too much! ☺

Drive to your nearby reservoir, river, lake or just a park. Do it for the sake of enjoying it, take pictures, capture your memories of the beautiful day that you can look back on during a not so beautiful day! Go for a drive on a spectacularly sunny day and roll the windows down. What??? No AC? That's right! Windows down, wind blowing through your hair, your favorite song playing, sing it at the top of your lungs! Why? Because you can!

The week before Christmas, load up your family or a few friends and go on a hunt for the best Christmas light displays! Drive through neighborhoods and check out the decorations, take pictures of your favorites to look at later. After you are finished, go back home and make hot chocolate, the really good kind, marshmallows, whipped topping, the whole nine yards! While you are sipping on that chocolaty goodness, look at the pics everyone took of their favorite lights.

I think you are beginning to get the feel for sunset chasing! It begins with sunsets, but it certainly does not end there. Each second we are given is a gift, each tic of the clock is another opportunity to live, love, laugh, care, cry, hug, and so much more!

May we all be in the #sunsetchasers club ... why?

Because we CAN!

8

GOD WINKS

Sitting in my doctor's office when I was initially diagnosed with "Ovarian Cancer that had spread", I experienced my first mind blowing experience. Dr. Haynes wanted me to be seen by Dr. Mahdi at Cleveland Clinic, as he is an Ovarian Specialist. He is in great demand and we were very concerned how soon I would be able to see him. The fact that she was able to get me in to him in two days was nothing short of a miracle! Being on this side of the situation, I can tell you that having Dr. Mahdi as my surgeon and Oncologist has made a world of difference for me both physically and mentally!

I begin this chapter with my Dr. Mahdi story because this was the first of countless events that could not be humanly explained. I remember so many times saying, "Wow, that's crazy, what are the odds of that happening?" Finally, I was reminded that these occurrences were not odd, they were completely GOD! These completely out of the blue events were simply God winks!

What is a God wink? The Lynn definition of a God wink is a surprising "coincidence" which really is not a coincidence at all! It is God's way of demonstrating His concern for each minute detail of our lives! God winks are some of the most exciting and miraculous events in our daily lives that we all too often overlook or mistake for a common coincidence.

This is the portion of the book where I wish that I could meet up with each one of you, one-on-one, and share some amazing stories with you. Since that is not possible, please allow me to simply share a few of my favorite and recent God winks with you right here!

My first opportunity to speak to a group regarding my book and my journey was at a Ladies Night Out, I referred to that in an earlier chapter. It was after that speaking engagement that a girl came up to me that I had not seen in probably twenty-five or more years! Angie and I attended the same Christian School, she was quite a bit younger than me, but it was a small enough school that everyone knew everyone.

Angie came up to me in tears as she relayed her story to me about her husband, Dave, and all of the cancer struggles he had endured. At first, my heart was utterly broken for this young family that had gone through such an immense cancer journey. After we reunited, shared several hugs, and committed to keeping up with and praying for each other, I realized something very important! This was a God wink!

God allowed Angie to come that evening in the midst of her insanely busy life, her sick husband and so many other factors that could have kept her home. He allowed me to speak about my journey which deeply touched Angie's life because of their struggles and fight. Who knows if the story shared that night would have affected her as much as it did if it had not come from someone she knew? The best part of this God wink is that Angie and I are good friends now, we text often and keep up with each other's lives. Most importantly, we are there to pray for and encourage one another each chance that we get!

The next speaking engagement was at a church that I attended when I was growing up. I had not been back there in years, it was a very rewarding experience to go back to my roots and share my journey with them. After the service I went back to my book table and a line quickly formed of folks who wanted to speak with me or purchase my book. A lady came up to me and had such a troubled look on her face. Suzanne introduced herself to me. She had such a kind face, we just seemed to immediately connect.

She explained how ironic it was that I came to speak on that day because the very next day one of her very best friends was going in for surgery. Not just any surgery, MY surgery, not just any diagnosis, Ovarian cancer, stage 4. May I continue? Her friend's surgery was going to be at Cleveland Clinic, her friend's surgeon was not just any surgeon, it was MY surgeon! We shared so many similarities! Suzanne just needed some encouragement and reassurance and I was so very grateful that God had placed me there at just the most opportunistic moment! She took my contact information and I sent a book for her friend Jan.

I was able to locate Jan on Facebook, then one by one her family connected with me as well. What an amazing family! Throughout Jan's surgery, treatments and journey, Jan and I kept very closely in touch via texting. After Jan had gotten to a point that she was strong enough to travel, she and her family offered to meet me for lunch. Through our efforts, one bright Sunday afternoon, this meeting happened! It was so incredible to meet up with Jan, her daughters, Tory and Tessa, and Jan's sister, Micki! We had such a wonderful meeting which felt more like a reunion with family I had not seen in a very long time. (Okay, I had never met them previously, but you certainly could not tell!)

Not only have we developed a sister-like closeness, Jan has also agreed to be one of my editors for this book! Jan has an enthusiasm that is contagious, a heart that is bottomless, an energy that is similar to the Energizer Bunny and a genuine sincerity that is very rarely seen or experienced. I am so inspired by and through her life, as well as the way she thrives through her journey!

Suzanne, Jan and I certainly realized quickly that this was not ironic or an amazing coincidence, it was a miraculous God wink! Okay, let's break this one down to let God show off for a second!

1. The timing of my speaking engagement there, THE DAY BEFORE Jan's surgery!

2. Suzanne was able to attend that service which was the BIG key!

3. I had a very similar diagnosis, same hospital, same surgery, same surgeon and same treatments!

4. I was able to connect with Jan and her entire family via Facebook!

5. We did not just GET in touch, we STAYED in touch!

6. We actually made the effort to get together with her family!

7. Jan accepted the challenge of being one of my editors for my book!

When you think about each piece of the above puzzle, without even one of these circumstance coming together, we would not be reading about this! Who made all of this come together, each minute detail? Only God could have orchestrated this!

I would love to tell you a little bit about Glenn. Sharon shared Glenn's journey with us on our POP (Power of Prayer) page on Facebook so that we could pray for him through each step of his extremely difficult cancer experience. As typically and wonderfully occurs, everyone rallied around Glenn with each update.

Glenn, through Sharon, requested several of my #inittowinit bracelets. He truly embraced the meaning behind the bands and wanted to share that with all of his friends and family. Throughout the past few months, I continued to share bracelets with him until ultimately he decided to create his own band. When Sharon brought Glenn's bracelet to me to wear, I was in tears as I saw the purple band. It was not only the same shade of purple that I used, (purple is the color that represents his cancer) but one of the sides was inscribed with #inittowinit ! I am so honored to share in this journey with Glenn and to share my motto with him, as well.

Finally, I would love to share about a man that I never had the honor to meet. This gentleman lived in Tennessee and had his own journey with cancer. My aunt and uncle gave him one of my #inittowinit bracelets and shared with him that I would be praying for him as well. Throughout his difficult days, he always had my bracelet on. I prayed that every time he put it on he would remember that someone in Ohio was praying for him and cheering him on through his darkest days!

His journey here on earth concluded with God calling Him Home… my aunt and uncle went to the funeral home for the calling hours. Much to their surprise, when they saw his body for the final time, he still had that bracelet on! I get very emotional each time I recall this story. A man in Tennessee I had never met was able to find hope and strength through a bracelet. The God wink here is that my sister and I were sitting in my surgeon's office processing the most intense news of my life when God gave me #inittowinit. Little did I know the inspiration the motto and verse would have on those I would never be able to meet here on earth, but, Oh! the reunion we will have in Heaven!

I hope this chapter gave you a bit of insight to only a few of the God winks that I have been blessed with in the past several months! God winks, He blinks, and so often we miss it! May we begin each morning with our eyes, hearts, and ears wide open to whatever God has for us! I no longer believe in coincidence or chance, instead I see God winking! I no longer use the word accident, but appointment, straight from the One who cares about each detail of my day. God is winking, do you see it?

9

FU MANCHU

There are certain things that will always stay etched in my mind, no matter how much time goes by. Giving birth to my amazing children, the last time I remember being with my grandparents, certain birthdays, and memories that will mean something special to me forever. One of these said times was when my sister and I were leaving my doctor's office after hearing the words "ovarian cancer". Not just hearing those words is memorable, but the song we heard in my sister's van immediately following that appointment: Tim McGraw, "Live Like You Were Dying!"

I always loved this song, I knew that it was inspired by Tim's father who passed away. I remember singing that song over and over again prior to my diagnosis. It seemed to take on an entirely new meaning after one doctor's appointment! For those of you who may not know this song, it talks about all of the things that this person wanted to do but did not do until he received a bleak diagnosis!

Before I was sick, I had ALWAYS wanted to write a book. Legitimately, my entire adult life I had the desire to put my thoughts down on paper and have it published. I love to write as it is therapeutic and thought-provoking for me. It is one of the ONLY ways that I am creative. Why did I not take the time to write a book before cancer? I suppose it just did not seem like an urgent matter, I would have time for that later, right? Then all of the sudden my security blanket was ripped out from under me and I decided that there was no better time than the present! What made me finally act on a life-long ambition? Please keep reading…

Since I was a young child, I always enjoyed seasons changing. I could not tell you which one is my absolute favorite, I could choose reasons for each! Living in northwest Ohio all of my life, we certainly do enjoy dramatic seasonal transitions. Sometimes two or three in one day! Okay, but seriously, I have always enjoyed those times of change. One of my favorites though is going from fall to winter and seeing the very first snowflakes.

When I was young, I would "frolic" in the first flakes! If the snow fell at night, morning, or afternoon, it made no difference, I would go outside and dance in the snow! I had not participated in frolicking in so many years until last year! I decided that at the first sight of the magical, white, fluffy flakes I was going to dance like no one was watching! Guess what? I did! I was at work and I saw the tiniest of twirling flakes begin to float down and I went out to our parking lot and danced around like a complete fool! Why had it taken me so long to fully embrace and enjoy this tradition from years past?

As much as I love seasons and the transitions between them, I also love the beach, the ocean, the sun and everything involved with a vacation surrounding these amazing things! I remember laying in Cleveland Clinic and my brother asking me if I could do anything or be anywhere at that very moment, what would I choose? Without hesitation I responded that I wanted to be on a beach, by the ocean, any beach and any ocean! We figured out that it had been nine years since I had taken the time to do that!

This past April, my parents and I journeyed to Myrtle Beach, South Carolina! We drove together and stopped at some nice spots on the way down. I still remember the feeling I had when we pulled into our hotel parking lot at Myrtle Beach. It was a beautiful day, not very warm, our hotel room was not ready yet, but I could not have been anymore excited! Mom walked down to the beach with me even though it was windy and cool. The moment I saw the ocean and felt the breeze that only comes off that vast body of water, it took my breath away!

Our room was on the fourth floor and was ocean front! The view from our room was something that I obviously could not get enough of. I took countless pictures just trying to capture that majestic view so that I could take it home with me. I will never forget the feeling I had each time I stepped into the hot sand and felt it between my toes. I will cherish the moment when I first stepped into the ocean and felt the waves hit my legs.

Why did I wait ten years to go to the ocean? Another question is why after waiting that long did I finally make the effort to go? Are you answering these questions in your own mind about things you long to do, places you desire to go, people you wish to visit? I hope so! There is a point to all of this!

One thing I have not mentioned yet is my "bucket list". Do you have one? I have recently been told that we need to call it my "life goals list" instead of my "bucket list". I can like that! Either way, I do have one! I have had one in my mind for a very long time. One of the things on that list is to go to Alaska! The pictures and movies I have observed from Alaska are some of the most beautiful scenes I have ever seen.

I have to mention another "life goals list" item here because it goes right along with this! Since I was a teenaged girl, my favorite Christian singer of all time has been Sandi Patty! Her voice, testimony, and her amazing personality have just always been so mesmerizing to me! Needless to say, even being able to sing on the stage with her would be a dream come true for me! So, next month, my life-long friend, Eunice and I are going on a cruise to Alaska with Sandi Patty! We even purchased the up-grade to allow me the opportunity to sing in a choir with her during a concert! WHAT??? I have to pinch myself when I think this is really going to happen!

I waited fifty-one years to go on a cruise to Alaska and get to sing back up to my favorite singer! I had never even looked into this type of trip before. In addition, I would have laughed if you had even hinted to the fact that I might be on a cruise with Sandi! Nonetheless, both of those things are happening next month!

I have shared a few of the exciting things that I have been blessed enough to get to experience or will soon. I have been asking you questions and telling you there was a distinct purpose to this chapter! Have you guessed what it might be? I hope so! Some of my favorite lyrics to the song that inspired this chapter is " I went sky divin', I went Rocky mountain climbin', I went 2.7 seconds on a bull named Fu Manchu!" I will always tease my sister as I reference this song and the fact that I still might ride that bull!

My purpose to this chapter is to urge my readers to LIVE LIKE YOU ARE DYING! Do what you want to do, what you love to do. Hug those family and friends that you cherish. Go visit your aunts, uncles and cousins. What is your favorite vacation spot? When is the last time you visited there? When is the last time you took a day off of work to actually have the DAY OFF? When is the last time that you frolicked or made a snow angel?

Our earthly life is too short, possibly shorter than any of us realize! Do you have a "life goals list"? If not, please start one today! Then, don't let it stop there! Making the list is only the first step! Make those things happen! Use each moment to make a memory! Today only comes around one time, you will never get this day back again! Treat today as a gift, it is the "present!"

My wish for you is that you will utilize the page I have placed in the back of this book for your launch pad to truly living! See if you can fill up that page with life goals that you may not have even considered before today! If you notice, there is a line to write a goal on, but there is also a place to check it off when you have made it happen! My prayer is that you will have as many checks as you do lines filled in. Who knows, you might even ride that bull named Fu Manchu?

10

LIFE LESSONS

The definition of the word *lesson* according to Wikipedia is*: a structured period of time where learning is intended to occur. It involves one or more students being taught by a teacher or instructor.* When I think about *life lessons,* I initially think about how difficult life can be! Therefore, life lessons must be extremely difficult as well! There is no doubt that these lessons can be quite complicated and even confusing at times! Look back at the definition though. We are being taught by a teacher or instructor, what a relief when I remember God is my teacher.

The most rewarding pieces of life lessons for me is the knowledge that my Instructor wants the best for me and He knows the beginning from the end! God knows the plans that He has for me, plans for welfare and not for calamity, to give me a future and a **hope**! (Jeremiah 29:11) These truths certainly make life lessons much easier to process, digest and hopefully, learn from!

I just want to take a few minutes and list some of the most life changing lessons I have been able to take with me as a result of the past fifteen months. I could literally write an entire book based on these truths, however fear not, I will briefly summarize! I included these in this book because after each speaking engagement, so many people would come up to me afterward and request a copy of this list. So, hang on, here we go!

1. **Google is NOT God!** Often times Google is the FIRST thing we turn to with our questions, am I right? Google, Siri, Alexa, etc... Here is the truth, none of these sources know everything! Each one can be very useful tools, without a doubt, BUT, it stops there. Hint: When it comes to cancer diagnoses, such as odds and percentages, search engines are NOT the final say and most often not worthy of researching. (Thank God for that!)

2. **God is NOT surprised!** What an immense and all-encompassing comfort! No matter what the day brings, even if it is something that completely blindsides us, take heart! God is never surprised, He's got us, every day and in every circumstance!

3. **God's ways are SO much higher than my ways!** I have learned to find great solace in the reality that I don't have to understand it all, I just need to TRUST in the One who does! I am still learning that re-calculating is not always a bad thing, I just have to trust in my GPS! (**G**od's **P**lan is **S**overeign)

4. **You have to FEED *faith* and STARVE *fear*!** Whatever we feed the most will reign in our lives! Starving fear is one of the greatest lessons I am striving to learn. The more malnourished the fear in

our lives becomes, the more energy and strength we have left over to feed our faith! If you want to go on a diet that will change your life for eternity? **STARVE FEAR!**

5. **God's grace IS enough!** We talk about this so often and yet how consistently do we apply this truth? No matter what, His grace **is** sufficient, it is MORE than sufficient. When we realize that our deficiency is made strong through His efficiency, what a difference it will make!

6. **My weakness shows off God's strength!** Not so long ago I was very ashamed of my weakness, I tried to hide it so that no one ever saw it. What a liberating truth to grasp, when I am weakest, **He is strongest!** I am extremely thankful that I finally learned that my story is NOT my story at all, it is HIS!

7. **Every day is a blessing and none of us know tomorrow!** I worked with one of the kindest men I have ever known while in Knoxville, Tennessee. His name is Bunny Oaks. Each day when he came into work he would say, "Good morning Lynn, how are you?" After I responded and asked him how he was doing, without fail his reply was, "Every day's a blessing!" I have never forgotten that, even on the most desolate day. EVERY day we are given is indeed a blessing! None of us know what tomorrow will bring, life can stop or change on a dime, but one thing we DO know is that EVERY day is a gift, a true blessing!

8. **Every trial has a silver lining!** Wow! What a life-changing statement! When we busy ourselves

looking for the silver lining in each trial, guess what it takes our eyes off of? THE TRIAL! So, when your trial seems almost too difficult to bear, get out that magnifying glass and start searching for the silver lining… it is there, I promise!

9. **Don't just live each day you are given, live it in HIGH DEFINITION, live it as if it is a gift, because it is!** Have you watched an analog TV lately? While my parents and I were on vacation in Myrtle Beach, our TV channels were definitely not in high definition. Our eyes quickly adjusted to the dull colors and lack of clarity. Once we returned home and back to our HD TV, it was almost shocking! The difference between the two are night and day! Try living in HD for just one week, I guarantee you, the results are such that you will never want to go back!

10. **Notice when "God winks" and tell Him how much you appreciate it!** May we keep our eyes, ears, minds and hearts open wide to these special circumstances that are God sends! (And then take time to acknowledge and thank Him for these winks and blinks!)

11. **Start and end each day being Forever Grateful and In It To Win It!** My entire outlook changed when I started living out my motto and not just reciting it or writing it with a hashtag in front of it! Living out and demonstrating forever gratefulness is a daily decision, it does not come naturally… at least not for me! Being #inittowinit is not something that "just happens" either, it takes a decision and choice each moment of the day to do whatever it takes to win. What is your definition of win? One definition

of this word is *to be successful or victorious in a contest or a conflict*. I embrace that definition! I hope you do as well!

Life lessons are only as valuable as what we learn from them. May we execute the application of those lessons in our daily lives. My heart's desire is that the lessons and truths that I am learning (yes, it is a daily process!) will be a help to your life, as well. After all, how valuable is the knowledge and experience we attain if we are not willing to share it with others?

God bless each of you in your journey through this thing called life. Thank you, from my heart, for coming along on mine! I leave you with one of my favorite Scripture verses: **Jeremiah 29:11** – *For I know the plans that I have for you, declares the Lord, plans for welfare and not for calamity to give you a* **future** *and a* **hope**!

Just to clarify, the title of my book is not merely a title. I am absolutely **STILL In It To Win It!!**

#forevergrateful   #stillinittowinit #Godisstillnotsurprised #livethedash #HDliving

11

LISTEN CLOSELY… IT WHISPERS!

Ovarian cancer is one of the most difficult and complicated cancers to detect. The symptoms are different for each person, yet there are similarities that often go unnoticed. The American Cancer Society has come out with updated data for 2018. It is estimated that there were 22,240 new cases of ovarian cancer in 2017. The deaths from those cases are 14,070 (63%). It is also estimated that 78% of ovarian diagnoses are Stage 3 before detection!

These numbers are staggering and sobering, so sad! Due to these statistics and my passion to spread ovarian cancer awareness, I have added this insert to my book.

A fact that may surprise you: **PAP tests do not show ovarian cancer**! Pelvic ultrasounds can detect ovarian tumors. There is a tumor marker called a CA (Cancer Antigen) 125 which is a blood test utilized in the diagnosis and management of ovarian cancer. A good rule of thumb is to see a Gynecologist once a year and to request one of the above tests if you have any concerns whatsoever.

Please look closely at this list of symptoms with the realization that each case is unique. This list is not inclusive of every symptom that someone might encounter, but these seem to be the more prevalent signs and symptoms. Please feel free to share this list with any female in your life, no matter her age.

1. Abdominal bloating
2. Feeling full quickly while eating
3. Fatigue
4. Menstrual changes
5. Abdominal or pelvic pain
6. Unexpected weight loss or gain
7. Urinary symptoms (urgency or frequency)
8. Difficulty eating or taking antacids frequently

If you or someone you know exhibits these symptoms persistently for two weeks or more, please make an appointment with your Gynecologist immediately.

Please listen to your body closely, ovarian cancer whispers! If you have questions or concerns or would like more information please feel free to visit the website: ovarianconnection.org or send an email to ovariancancerconnection@yahoo.com.

#noonefightsalone #itstimetogetrealaboutteal

My Life Goals List
(*Fu Manchu*)

Activity/Event   **Check Off!**

`1.

_____

2.

_____

3.

_____

4.

_____

5.

_____

6.

_____

7.

_____

8.

_____

9.

_____

10.

_____

11.

_____

12.

_____

13.

_____

14.

_____

15.

_____

16.

_____

17.

_____

18.

_____

19.

_____

20.

_____

Your Song

First Verse:

You were dealt a life changing blow;

You gave it your all, this we know.

Cancer, not what we wanted to hear;

Only God knows the pain it brought, the fear.

You didn't bow your head for very long;

Instead you looked up and found your song.

Chorus:

Your song was love,

Your song was peace;

Your song was strength;

It gave such sweet release.

God knew you had taken it all;

Until the day you heard Him call.

Second Verse:

We saw your hope, in spite of your pain;

We watched you dance right through the rain.

Some would have fallen beneath this weight,

Some would have given up, accepted their fate.

You faced the storm and fought to the end;

You taught us to be brave, never break, only bend.

Chorus:

Your song was love,

Your song was peace,

Your song was strength,

It gave such sweet release.

God knew you had taken it all,

Until the day you heard Him call.

Third Verse:

God saw you fight just like a champ; He was with you all the way;

We knew you earned your time to rest; we said all we wanted to say;

Finally, God called you home; rest well our hero, while we're apart;

You're with us every second, always in our heart.

Chorus:

Your song is love,

Your song is peace,

Your song is strength;

It gives us sweet release.

God knew it was your time to go;

We miss you more than you can know.

Reprise:

Your song brings us joy;

Your song brings us peace;

We'll keep singing your song;

It gives such sweet release.

We'll sing your song, each sweet refrain;

While in our hearts, you will remain.

We'll sing your song, along our way,

'Til we sing it with you again, some day.

LMS 4/12/18

Lynn Michele

ABOUT THE AUTHOR

Lynn Michelle Salyer was born in Sandusky, Ohio and has lived most of her life in Fremont, Ohio.

Lynn has two children. Leisha is 28 years old and is married to Tim Chism. Luke is 26 years old and is married to Ali, they were blessed with Lynn's first grand baby on May 15th, Emery Rose! Lynn's children, grandchild and family mean absolutely everything to her!

Loving and serving the Lord are very important to Lynn as she depends on Him daily for her strength, healing and power.

Lynn is the author of *In It To Win It* and *Still In It To Win It.*

Lynn is an avid Ohio State Buckeyes, Pittsburg Steelers and LeBron James fan!

Ever since being diagnosed with advanced Ovarian Cancer in 2017, Lynn has a heart and compassion for anyone who is facing this furious foe! Lynn is one of the founders of the Ovarian Cancer Connection's Fremont chapter. This organization is staffed by all volunteers, thus 100% of the money raised goes to assisting local ladies with Gynecologic Cancer. OCC helps with gas cards for treatments, utilities, personal needs, and other resources.

Lynn has had several speaking engagements surrounding her first book and continues to donate that book to any cancer patient with whom she comes into contact.

In addition, she consistently goes back to the Sandusky Cancer Center to visit chemo patients and try to spread encouragement, joy and hope to those who need it most!

Lynn is involved with Survivors Teaching Students. This national organization goes to Colleges and Universities and speaks to classes of future RN's about the signs and symptoms of Ovarian Cancer. She has an enormous desire to spread awareness regarding one of the most deadly and misdiagnosed diseases.

If you are interested in having Lynn come to your church, ladies group or cancer fund raiser to speak, please contact her at inittowinitbooks@gmail.com or go to her Facebook page Inittowinitsilverlining.

Made in the USA
Middletown, DE
17 January 2020